Pas[illegible]
Arca[illegible]ia
Close

Joan McGavin

Oversteps Books

First published in 2017 by Oversteps Books Ltd
6 Halwell House
South Pool
Nr Kingsbridge
Devon
TQ7 2RX
UK

www.overstepsbooks.com

ISBN 978-1-906856-68-7

Printed in Great Britain by imprint digital, Devon

for Charlie

Acknowledgements

Some poems here were among those commissioned by Hampshire County Council and the Hampshire Cultural Trust while I was Hampshire Poet 2014. These were the war poems *Learning how to throw bombs* and *Generation Gap* (the latter published as a bookmark). *Books are good for you* was also commissioned, and published as a postcard disseminated across Hampshire libraries.

To accompany an Arts Council travelling exhibition of Henry Moore lithographs, the poem *Stone Writing* was commissioned – and shown alongside a lithograph owned by Hampshire County Council that was included in the Winchester Discovery Centre exhibition.

Versions of *Burning* and *The Operation of Air* were used alongside films of fire and air as part of the Elemental Dialogues project (See www.annacady.com and https://elementaldialogues.wordpress.com/)

The Dressing-gown was published in 'The Book of Love and Loss: Poems for Today' (edited R V Bailey and June Hall; The Belgrave Press, Bath, 2014).

Some of the poems in the 'High Road' section were written during a residency I had in 2012 as a Hawthornden Fellow.

Outside Lecture Room 5 was a prizewinner in the 2013 High Cross House poetry competition.

I am grateful to Stephen Boyce for reading a draft of this volume and for all his advice and encouragement.

Contents

Salt

The changing taste of rivers
told me where I was heading.
How could I fail to swim faster?
I'd hugged the coast for hours,
kept the lap of landbound waves
to my right, where the tang of fresh water
mixed in with salt would flood
the roof of my mouth
at each estuary.

At night I dozed in the hammock between waves
or beached and slept away from houses
but within earshot of tides.

Sometimes the pull of the land
sometimes the roll of the waves
sometimes the taste of the salt
changing, were not enough:
I'd let myself sink down
and rest on the sea bed
among stones. Sometimes
I needed all my surfaces
to be inside water.

When I came ashore,
the salt drained out of me,
my mouth was emptied

and my legs grew
into the rhythm of
what they call walking.

Portrait of the Ferryman

A man is dreaming
of the beautiful, naked woman
whose face he can't make out
                                        and of the cottage
they'll live in where you open
the door and the sound of the sea dances in.

*

A man is praying
that the mad woman he has married
will be cured if they go
                                        to the village
on the bay where the tide whispers
only healing words.

*

A man is sighing.
He can only kill the woman
slowly, from her head downwards.
                                                  The people she visits
in the houses inland murmur at it
but stay indoors, don't know how to save her.

*

The man is blind,
his thoughts fine embroidery.
The woman whose face he's never seen
                                                  creates a world for him
day by day, unbounded by the walls
of their cottage in sight of the sea.

*

The man is dead
and in a lace-lined coffin.
The woman he loved predeceased him
                                        and the house they lived in
is falling into the sea,
weeping rocks.

*

There's a dark river
that connects them all:
the naked, lolling woman,
the man with closed eyes and sunken cheeks,
the plain, single-storey houses in the hollows
and on the hillside, the rocks
that keep marching towards the water
but haven't moved an inch in aeons
and the screams and songs blotted
by such white, white sand.

The Ash Waif

for Janet Hadley Williams

We took the ash waif in. She was no trouble.
Lived quietly in her bedroom, but was sociable, too:
made good conversation at mealtimes, said she was
from a country far away, near an island
where huge pine trees grew, a million years old.

She kept an eye on the weather reports,
the state of the ash, by slipping inside her laptop.
Those who'd flown her here couldn't take her home
yet. She worried. When she fed us stories, though,
we called it quits. They were rent enough, we said.

Soon we were sitting at her feet of an evening
as words bubbled out of her
in that voice she used
to tell us about an admirer in the far country —
and sure enough a blazon of flowers arrived one day:
forget-me-nots, orchids, bright rags on black stems we didn't
know the names of. When she flew away

they were there, still, in her room —
heavy to bring downstairs, like carrying
a glacier bristling with colour.

Of the ash waif only this much remained:
the bouquet, hairs on her pillow,
and beside her bed across a scrap of paper
in what we took to be her handwriting
the word Eyjafjallajökullsdottir.

Delivery Men

Crowd saves toddler from five-storey fall: news headline, 21/6/2013

Who was savvy enough
to catch the scene on camera,
knowing it was one
that would go viral?
Not the delivery men of Ninghai
who saw her cling
to a fifth floor ledge
and knew she would fall.

Who thought only of themselves,
ignored the common bond
that means we save our own —
especially the young of the species?
Not the delivery men of Ninghai
who moved close to each other,
stretching their arms
in the seconds it took
to *do something!*

Who will never forget
that alleyway, the thing
they were all part of?
Who will recall it
in their bleakest times?

Who will never regret —
when an arm pains them
(a rheumatic where a bone
snapped) —
their prompt clustering?

And who will recall
the moment the toddler
moved on the ground at their feet,
the moment of knowing
she was unharmed?

And who will remember
the delivery men?

Who will go on watching?

The Tribulations of a Venetian Merchant

Setting out from Venice on the first day of the year,
it's 1245 — yet when he reaches Florence
it's 1244. Days later he fetches up in Pisa
where 1246 has started.
He catches his breath, decides
to go on westwards.
In Provence it's 1245 again.
He goes on into France, arrives before Easter,
finds he's once more (he can't ignore it)
back in 1244.

In mediaeval times you could tell where you were,
but not always *when*. Historians can explain it.
And of course, there was nothing in the way
of what's available today
in Milwaukee General Mitchell Airport:
a place labelled *Recombobulation Area.*

Lucca

Receding, their voices reach back to her:
Grazie, grazie — with a coda of giggles.
They casually confer
on a breathless
tourist
who's managed at last
to heft their lost football
up and over the city wall to them
the freedom of Lucca.

The Gleam

Hendrickje Stoffels looks at Rembrandt's A Woman Bathing in a Stream

It's hard to imagine the sensation
of water when you're not in it.
He'd said I was to keep still,
imagine I was still in water,
going deeper, holding my shift
up out of the wet.
I was worrying over
so much of my legs showing
when what I just then felt
was the baby quickening
the flutter of it swimming
in the stream inside me.

He said he liked the way
I looked down — to keep that expression —
though I didn't say what it was
brought the soft look
to my eyes. He's caught
it, right enough,
with his clever, dabbing brush.
And later I thought

I suppose a painting's like
a baby for him
or like trying to deepen the gleam
the more you polish
a copper kettle, a brass fender.
It takes time to get there:
months and months of it.

High Sierra

As the hang glider drifted down
into the high sierra village
so remote that strangers seldom found it

the old woman crossed herself, reminded
of invading soldiers in the valleys below — what they'd done
to her and her sister. The boy with arms and legs
no bigger than a toddler's restrained
an impulse to run over and touch the wings.
He was used, already, to curbing desires.
The man cobbling shoes near the open door
of his shop glanced up, a nail
between his lips, looked down
at his last quickly, went back to work.
And the bag-of-sugar baby? What she saw was
a dark mass between her and the sun, moving earthwards,
and it didn't smell of milk.

Giving up Green

After we surrendered
they took our weapons,
insisted we give up green.
It was unknown on their planet
and they wanted it for themselves.

It started with flower stems —
the blooms collapsed earthwards
like butterflies settling.
Ferns went next, and mosses,
things that grow under trees.

With trees themselves still green
we ignored the thieving.
When each tree's leaves had gone,
we saw the threat they posed —
did what we could then:

resistance groups with trip-wire,
barbed wire, whatever we could get.
None of it worked.
Of the destruction done
they said nothing publicly:

the bulldozed forests,
stolen hills, grubbed-up
meadows, our parks taken
and turned
into hardstanding.

When I found some camomile
they had somehow missed,
I pushed down hard, tried to draw
green into me, save it, madly,
through the soles of both feet.

Joyce and the Swan

Imagine the girl who loved diving
coming up from the depths
of the Ouse at Wolverton
to a large swan
between her and the bank –
her scaredy-cat classmates
already scrambled ashore.

As he neared, her only option
was, she thought, to swim over,
lean two hands, thumb to thumb,
where his neck
turned into body. And push hard.
What she talks about now, ninety years on,

is how soft the down
was, how her hands
sank in and in.

The Uses of Metal*

Metal will save my head, John Bradshaw thought,
as he strode into Westminster Hall for the trial.

Metal will shield my heart, he hoped,
touching the breastplate under his robes.

Metal could kill a king, he knew,
condemning Charles Stuart to the block.

Metal would hold his own body, dug up,
put into chains when the new king came
— the one who ordered

that Bradshaw's corpse be beheaded.
They skewered his skull on a metal pike,

with Cromwell's and Ireton's,
at Westminster, for all to see.

**The Judge John Bradshaw, who presided at the trial of Charles 1, fearing for his safety, wore a hat lined with metal, and armour under his robes. After the Restoration, his disinterred body was posthumously executed, by beheading.*

Above and Below

near and in Rosslyn Chapel

Rain set in for the day
washes the trees even greener

beads the pink globes draped
over rhododendrons

as if to celebrate

the two hounds Help and Hold
asleep seven hundred years.

Nothing to see in the crypt
apart from five or six angels.

Panicked

at Hawthornden

On the phone as I walk through
heavy rain, up the long drive,
I'm surprised by deer, first two

larger, then a small one arrives
with a stumble, leaps back
out of my path, dives

towards me again with such a lack
of certitude that it veers
all ways at once, then taken aback

goes headlong under trees, careers
over grass, to disappear
as fast as it can into the sheer

encroaching dark. Near,
in the hollow where the hind
couched, grass springs up clear

of the ditch, and, halted, I find
the aura of three gentle panics
is here, and gone, behind

the oaks — and your voice
is in my hand
human,
insistent.

The Presence of Steeplejacks

at Hawthornden

We hear their over-and-aboveness.
They're busy with slates, rooftree.
Like window-cleaners, they don't look *through*.
Their words, instead, float round,
slip, often fully formed,
in at open windows,
surprising us.

At dusk they leave their ladders
barred across with spars
tied on with bright blue rope.
Why? we wonder, looking up.
— To deter midnight Mohawks
on a tour of Europe's high spots?
We're certainly not tempted.

Their bucket hangs down,
between rungs and roof,
then the ladder's clinched
to spire with four stout ropes,
each thicker than the one above,
less being needed
to hold a rung snug
as the spire narrows.

The young steeplejack undoes them
daily, leans out wide
to shoo away the birds
once he's finished the phone-call
which he makes
(it's a point of honour)
with phone held just where
the chimney-stack meets sky.

Instructions for Swimming in a Sea Loch

Loch na Keal, Mull

Look at the water.
While mountains stand round

step in where the sea
has crept up on them

and the gold light of late
afternoon bends down, benign,

to contemplate this landscape
of islands and gaps

you're moving through.
Wait till your feet ankles

calves are used
to the cold, take time

until, much deeper,
you've warmed the water

around. Now reach out
with your arms

push off from
the last toehold

on land
let go

of upright
tip the horizon

swim.

Facing Staffa

a riddle in three similes

Something small
between the newspaper
and my face as I sit outside
tries to read
what I'm reading
traces along the words
like an adult's finger
touching under each
to help a child cope.

I start back; it moves off
begins inspection duty
like a security guard
checking door and window
behind me, following
the angle of each —
Is it locked?
Is it snug in its frame?

— before flying off,
round the building, inland,
towing its sound
behind it, insistent,
like an outboard motor
far off across the sea loch
and unseen.

Answer: a damselfly

West Highland Gothic

See how a black crack zigzags to meet
the window's corner like scars on a boxer's face.

See through another window a brown case sits
full of green-furred forks, one bone-handled knife, as if a child
playing 'travelling salesman' got bored, up and left.

See where half a window has gone; inside, an old-fashioned TV
stares blankly out at the sea as if, in a fit of pique,
it turned its back on the room.

See through a broken window, a mattress on a metal bedframe
in a far corner, curved, like that wave in the Hokusai print

and in the room to its right a splintered floorboard sticks up
at an angle — a prop in a comic film awaiting a footfall.

See where, round the side, a monster tree grows flat to the ground,
crowds towards the wall. Dusty nettles punctuate the garden

and the burn that gives the house its name ignores everything
but its headlong rush to the bay through culvert and bush.

A door's glued shut like a black eye at the wrong angle;
through that window a bow-fronted cabinet has glass intact,
but, bereft of china, stands, its back to the wall.

Looking through to the ledge there's a yellowed page
of the West Highland Free Press;
you can just make out the headline *Unspeakable Crimes.*

A disquisition

on the behaviour of these islands
should mention
how they creep closer overnight;
also, in the evening, recede
into the mist like a shy friend
going back behind her eyes.

It could make much of
how one of them can cast the others
into the shade when light
selects it and it glows
or how some shape-shift,
not enough to make you confuse them with others –
only a hill a little rounder, a strand
pencilling out longer into the sea –
and how this can apply also to their points
of recognition: the perfect vertical
at the Fingal's Cave end of Staffa
some days not being quite perpendicular
or another island developing a straight
up-and-down end also, not there before.

It should refer to
how they some days float
on the water as if plonked down
as God, distracted
during some other act of creation,
muttered *That bit of sea's not too crowded.*
Let's leave them there in the meantime

and should not ignore
how human things like an anemometer,
ruined or whole houses, a wind turbine,
a sheep fank, fail spectacularly
to hold them down,
appear like half-sprung nails
in a badly made boat.

Their ongoing relationship with clouds
is also worthy of mention
as is their ability to play
Grandmother's Footsteps –
but I repeat myself – something they never do.

Golf Hotel. January 7th 2015

The corporate art on the bar walls —
animals that require recognition,
poised between cave painting
and out-of-focus photographs — conveys
nonetheless the distance this inside
achieves from encroaching suburb
or cleat-pressed field where the eighteenth
could be where you reach into a hole
to find *anything*. Rain has blinded
the windows for days. It's not Paris,
but a sense
of terrorists let loose strides inside.

Rosewell on a wet June afternoon

is much like other
Lothian mining towns,
now mining's gone:
a grid of streets,
single-storey, terraced houses,
most neat, some not so neat
with rotten wood round windows
and maintenance undone;
bigger houses, too,
with sandstone walls,
down drives;
a miners' club in
utilitarian brick;
a church or two
(one quite striking)
and signs for parks,
so parks exist.
A douce silence pervades
the grayish gloom.

And something called The Institute
that even in this not-quite-town
shows 'aspiration' –

a thought that in the now strong rain
keeps me walking.
And when I see it,
it's grand:
a place where books once were
and may be still

and I thought of you saying how
wherever you went in the world
if you found a library
and could go in
you felt at home,
you felt as though light
was around you.

Stone Writing

from a Henry Moore lithograph

Static but always becoming something
else: instruments, pierced stones
containing space, fantastic animals.
What do you see in us?
A guitar, a gondola, a griffin,
a pair of lovers, stretched out, lounging?
Your own imagination, mirrored back?

To the right, writing:
in us you decipher lines
on a long, meandering walk,
a signature not wanting to be read,
calligraphy, ruined maps, crazy
cursive some turn their backs on.
What does this secret script say?

Questions, questions —
when we're supremely answers —
content to be
even if you see in us
proto-troikas, hollow cellos
played on by the air
between.

Pevsnering

a found poem

Varied, but not disciplined. Rusticated.
Perp details, churchy, rather ostentatious
and very conservative. Alas rather gimmicky.
Badly damaged by rabbits.
Two chamfers dying into the imposts.
Flowing tracery with small infillings.
One would like to know the sculptor.
Quite a powerful east frontage. Together
they make a distressing hotchpotch.
The two both hold on to a vine
which has brought forth not only grapes
but also their five children, their heads
and busts arranged fanwise. Rather tamely
neo-Jacobean. A puzzle, if ever there was one.
Impressive at first but soon recognized
as the last gasp of Otranto and Fonthill.
Gothic and unfortunate.

Sleeping with the Novel

for Carole Burns

Chapters further up
my vertebral column
follow on from those
in my lumbar region.
Behind my intestines —
all eight or so yards of them —
the plot thickens.

I lie with my back to it,
try to blank from my mind
how it's up there on the wall
with its typefaced eyes.

Does it want my sinews
to flesh out its characters?
My blood as ink
to go on writing itself?

This won't do!
I say out loud
as I turn and settle
on the low-set bed.
The air I displace
makes a Mexican wave
of a hundred white ghosts.

Loulan revisited
i.m. Ron Hansford

Skilful, mischievous,
you'd drop them into lines
like chillies into salad –

the kind of words your poems
sent me in pursuit of:
endorheic, exorheic.

Or you'd place them, carefully,
like a bricklayer working
in *Flemish or Dutch bond.*

Mr Grigg, who came to help
when we lived in the Polygon
told tales of bull headers, closers,

how many bricks it took
to build a semi, how, in India,
on a tea plantation,

he saw a woman toss her breast
over her shoulder so as to feed
her baby as she went on

picking leaves. (You would have
loved his language, the Hampshire
vowels rolling off his tongue.)

Should we have believed him?
Gravity seemed against it –
and gravity has got you now

though words like *harmattan*
breeze through your poems
and on into our heads,
never to desert us.

Advice to a student

who asked about when and how to write

In the morning, feeling as fine and fragile
— which really means as *strong* — as bone china,
in a sunlit room, sitting up in bed;
in a cave, sopping wet underfoot,
understanding at last the word *saturated*;

on an electronic notepad,
with the pen on a chain in your local bank,
with the gold pen that signed a peace treaty;

in a ruled school jotter,
on your parking ticket, betting slip, tablet,
on your deportation letter,
on your hospital appointment note,
in the expensive saddleworn leather book
kept especially for the purpose,
in that space on your tax form, for official use only;

on a bar of soap,
on toilet paper,
on the walls of your cell,
with your own blood
that will, through time, look brown.

Not
on your death certificate
in copperplate or any kind
of cursive.

Apprenticeship

Normandy, May 2013

I make myself listen
to how an old quarry
overgrown by greenery
is a beaker for birdsong.

A jet passes,
supersonically
wedges a pain into my head.

Without missing a beat
the birds continue.
They've heard it all before:

invaders' boots
cows complaining of udders
brimheavy with milk
rook-scarers that explode again
the minute you've forgotten them.

If only I could write poems
the way they go on singing.

If only I could learn — anything:
a beakful of tunefulness,

the larks' light, long
and lovely lineation.

Books are good for you

'A book must be the axe for the frozen sea within us'. Franz Kafka, 1904

Everyone knows it. They make you feel better.
Now doctors prescribe them — in script or in letter.

Read Shakespeare and poems for their curative powers
or seek out a book group, spend hours and hours

with doses of Hamlet or downing some rhyme.
But no matter your taste, it can help to spend time

in a way that de-stresses, that calms or consoles
or helps you imagine alternative roles

in life to those that you normally play.
We thought it already; researchers now say:

pick up those axes — those books, bless their makers,
unfreeze the seas, join the movers and shakers

who waltz with words, who dance on the floes —
stretching hands across ice so the chain of us grows.

Outside Lecture Room 5

I'm sitting in a corridor empty
apart from tables pushed against walls

between lecture room doors and I'm surprised
how comfy it is to be here, my back

to the wall, waiting for a meeting
to close. Although the building

seems old, its paintwork unhappy, some new
green diktat means the lights go out

every three minutes or so — as I stay still
in my pocket of space. All I have to do

to cure the darkness is wave the paper
I'm writing these words on; I can play

God by raising in an arc
my folded A4, wondering if all I actually

have to do is think *Let there be*

Primer

We both are known
by a no-nonsense mono-
syllable. When it comes to the heart
of the matter, though, we've grown
so close over the years our names
seem to morph nearer, too:
Joan and John — like children
in a 50s reading primer,
who smile, uncomplicated,
as the world outside
their room, with its gay gingham
curtains, its clear-faced kitchen clock,
gets ready to change.

Learning how to throw bombs

came after bridging, boat-construction,
cutting brushwood hurdles
for revetting trenches,
how to make wire entanglements –
all of this *field engineering*;
then map-reading, use of,
how to strip and reassemble
a Vickers gun. They'd all
made notes for that one.

When in the crater he cradled
his head, having lobbed
his practice hand-grenade,
he noted nothing at all
till, bayonet-sharp, it came:
a memory of being inspected,
briskly, during drill,
by three small, friendly,
stray French dogs.

An Officer Cadet, Artists Rifles, France, 1916

Generation Gap

With the Armistice declared,
school was closed
and the children all
ran hilty-skilty
down the brae.
Mum burst into the house —
her brother's photo
already three years
on the mantelpiece.

Newly
promoted corporal,
he holds
the swagger stick
self-consciously,
glances to the side.

And now she's gone,
and those questions
one could ask about him
— dead on the Somme —
will need books,
the internet, research,
for any hope of answers —
and between me and my uncle
only the red hair
and my mother
forever saying
how much I reminded her of him.

Even now

the phrase
men who march away

retains a trace of glamour
as if by going straight

down the Avenue and on board
troopships they were bound

not for France but faeryland
— with an 'e' — as if they'd never

end up in mud or as names
on walls, but rather walk back

into their old lives, except grown
firmer-jawed, filling the room more

and wearing, each of them,
a world-weary smile

of invitation
we'd simply know

how to respond to.
Even now.

What the Red Devil

might have thought was
that it was an anti-birth

this leaping and falling
with a D-Day survivor

strapped to his front
outside his wombless body

already held to him
by all the forces of the air

a labour of love so quick
the pangs were shared

by both of them. Not Venus
rising from the foam

an old man borne out of the sky
towards a quietened beach.

Armistice Day Rant

They died and we munch pizza
on Friday nights after work.
They died and we rev our way
onto cross-channel ferries
and can have muzak
wherever we go.
They died and we walk and talk
cheek by jowl on mobile phones.
We hear tannoyed voices that tell us
about delays and difficulties due to derailments

and we sit in darkened cinemas listening
while ears are sliced to the sound of music
and the sound of music endlessly tells us that
the hills are alive with the sound of music.

They died.
In exchange for two minutes of our silence
they give us all of theirs.

On such a day

*15th April 2015**

On such a day
you can imagine
how every piece of litter
on motorway verges leading here
turned to primroses.

On such a day
you can imagine
how each blackened sheet
from a burnt book
drifted back to reunite itself
with its spine

and that every creature —
magpie, fox, badger —
rose up, renewed,
looked at the car
that made it roadkill
then turned away
into the trees.

On such a day
you can imagine
a kind of beauty
in the sweating, middle-aged
lycra-clad bodies
of the cycling club members
crowded into Mr Bun the Baker's teashop
in Church Stretton.

And on such a day
you can imagine
the dead of Bergen-Belsen lined up,
shoulder to shoulder,
all along the top of the Long Mynd
with their faces turned up to the sunlight
as its warmth enters their bones
and the spring breeze passes over them.

** 15th April 2015, the 70th anniversary of the liberation by Allied troops of the death camp at Bergen Belsen, was the hottest day of the year so far.*

The Operation of Air

Glow-worms   punctuate it.

Pages loop over in it, hurry after each other
like impatient lovers. Prayer shawls unwrap
themselves in it. A cat will look at the space
in it that she intends to jump through.

As air moves curtains you glimpse green, you can see
either beyond, or not beyond, you can be stalled
at the flickering, the filling, will-o'-the-wisping,
the quivering and shivering, billowing.
How many words for its movement?

And air can be like fire: a good servant
but a bad master.
The gentle breeze, the passing current —
the one that poets would call a zephyr —
caresses and strokes
whatever it touches, a tentative lover,
while its big cousin, the tempest
uproots trees, plucks up whole villages
and dumps them elsewhere.
He's a thug, a bully, a gangster
who started off small,
once no more than a draught
that moved a cobweb or a curtain
or prompted a memory.
                                        Only by how it operates
on other things will you know it, will air show its
presence ...
and all memories are like air moving
through cobwebs

... or like tree shadows behind flimsy curtains.
They can be precise, but enigmatic,
memories of the so long ago past.

In dreams they group and gather,
glimmer or gutter.
As we wake they recede like breath
leaving the lungs of the dying.

***

Air warms more and more urgently,
till the worlds' angles, angularities, start to
collapse, are rolled up
to be bundled and tossed
out into the streets
or beyond barbed wire
boundaries.

An Everyday Fairy Tale

for Brian

An everyday heart I'd conjure
for you to find in the garden shed
by chance, one afternoon.

Unbroken, its own talisman,
full purse, you'd come across
it still beating, and spare.

You'll hurry it to hospital,
straight into the room
where masked retainers

will fit you with it.
You'll get your breath back.
You'll dance till dawn.

After watching a film about kites, projected onto the inside of a drawer

The languor, the languorousness
of kites. Time fell off the sky;
the kites caught it,
fished it out of the drawer
it had landed in,
towed it, stunned, back towards high,
their trailing ribbons
question-marking
the sky.

Time was dazed and hazy,
a half-wakened child
lured upwards
by avuncular, brightly clad
abductors.

No; too sinister
a metaphor.
Time, fallen into that drawer,
regressed to babyhood
and the kites
pretended to be storks
in illustrations
in old children's books,
delivering it.

Shocking

Oh, to be a young spider
at the peak of one's web-making powers
and all one's legs beautiful.
How sexy, how clever
to have made one's own trampoline
of light and dew, to bounce on daily,
to have a mossy branch for a horizon
and to have brought to a high
state of perfection
one's grab and smash
talents, one's use
of those electrical properties
that, according to an article
in *Naturwissenschaften*,
make the glue on one's web
shockingly effective.

The Boy from the Barracks

When I at last answered Big Boy back
he spat at me.
It dribbled over my left cheekbone.
I wanted to wipe it off
with the back of my hand
except I didn't want it
on any other part of me.

He was a boy from the Barracks.
It was a turf war over the old garages
where we Terrace kids played football,
started off our games of Hide and Seek.

Coming-ready-or-not
he and his gang had materialised
over the brow of the hill, like Red Indians —
except there was no hill and they weren't
on horseback.

We were chicken, didn't want a fight
so we walked — in slow motion — silently
round the corner towards our homes
as if to speak would unleash something.

I was the straggler — the one
they picked off at the pass,
trained their sights on,
fired their words at —
except he moved on from words
to spit.
Was there enough of it to drip,
I wondered, when it reached
the bottom of my face?

**

I hope Wee Hard Man grew up,
lives somewhere with a bit of greenery about it.
I hope someone loves him
and he found himself able to love them back
— and I hope he's given up spitting.

Pantomime's End

Just when we thought that political correctness had bitten
the dust
of the stage once and for all, with the dame's last gag
in a wildly outré series
about female late-life urinary incontinence,
there's the final transformation: all manner of things are well:

the villain abjures the service of giants; Jack says it's the
girl herself
who's gorgeous, roly-poly *or* slimline version; the king gets
his castle back;
the dame enters — she's put off her gash-of-lipstick,
rouge-cheeked mask —
and behold! a cross between Superman and Elvis in
white lamé madly
thrums his silver guitar. We're magicked up from our seats,

join in with the chorus, the dancers, youngsters
whose energy stops just short of manic. As if our lives
depend on it,
we're singing along with the pop classic I find I remember,
word for word, every aching syllable, *Oh, yes, I do!*

Civil and Military in the Loire Valley

Supping beer, some bikers sit circled
in a spot where *the ideas and intuitions*
of Leonardo, by turns civil and military engineer,
take shape before one's very eyes:
down the slope, among the trees, *giant*
and actionable machines await us visitors.

We're in Clos Lucé, where the *Tuscan genius*
would die, a friend of kings. A stone-carved coat-of-arms,
handled by angels, stares blankly towards Amboise
across the valley, and at me across the garden,
at the bikers' table next to mine,
lively with North-of-England banter.

Though I don't yet know it, tonight
les motocyclistes de l'Europe will rev
through the *environs* of Tours to their convention
and tomorrow, at breakfast, by the croissants
I'll bump into a massive French biker,
set his chunky silver chains chinking.

He'll surprise me with
Pardon, madame, his neat tiptoe aside.

Boomers and Spoils

The spoils of war — the one our parents survived,
even, we could see, at times enjoyed — lay about us
as we grew: a wandering step, a stretch,
a climb or rummage away.

I found a gun in the glory-hole
one day, when I went snooping —
in behind the toffee tin that rattled with screws
and wing-nuts. Not like the Colt 45s
in Ian's cowboy comics. It was shorter,
fatter, stubby, but definitely a gun
and so heavy, cold in my hand
I put it down pronto.
(For flares, I later learned. It explained why
there were no big bullets to go with it.)

You found, at your gran's, in Glasgow,
the samurai sword at the side of the wardrobe
and were allowed to hold it, on top of your hands,
as if presenting it to an Emperor
who'd arrived in Riddrie.
When I asked if it were ever unsheathed,
you said *Yes, when no-one was looking*,
went on to tell me about the twelve-
bore shotgun on the other side
of the wardrobe, next to the Saltire.

All of this, like the silver fox fur Dad had smuggled
back from Norway, worn round his waist,
that my mother wore for weddings, for special,
was how we came to glamour, to danger.
I wore the fur, sometimes, for fun.
It smelled of moth-balls, was the softest thing
I'd felt — then or ever since.
But I was frightened of the look in its hard glass eyes,
how its legs, tipped with claws, draped over my shoulders,
how it tapped, when I moved, against my Liberty bodice.

The Dressing-gown

Not to be shamed
by the old and tatty dressing-gown
she wore, for comfort,
in her own home —
here being public,
here the domain
of those who judge
by appearance —
urgent, in her hospital bed,
during that last illness,
she gave me an order.

Knowing her mindset
I bought the best I could:
quality above style
but colourful, completely lined
in cotton, made in England.
We called it her
'coat of many colours'
and smiled with her
at how grand she looked.

Later, I wore it myself, sometimes,
on cold and sleepless nights.

It's been years.
Today, I've decided,
is the day I wrap it up
for the charity shop.
I know I can hand it over.
I know I'll be able
just to walk away,
not to say
Give it a good home, please:
some old lady
who's had a hard life,
like my mother's —
an old lady who wakes up cold.

Irritable Reaching

Negative Capability, that is, when a man is capable of being in uncertainties, mysteries, doubts, without any irritable reaching after fact and reason.

Keats

She must have pulled a muscle.
That was how it felt.
It had been too late, really, to go
planting daffodils
on the first day of December.

Her fingers met something round, hard,
the size, it felt, of a tennis ball
that the bath hadn't soaked away.
She called her lover for a second opinion,
some words that might comfort.

The blue-shirted consultant ignored her,
spoke to his students only. He was like a spider
touching a particularly nasty, small fly.
She wanted to bat him away.
Much later, the tennis ball gone

and tubes coming out of her,
draining into bottles,
words like 'supply and demand'
and 'the circulation of the lymph'
buzzed round her.

No-one seemed to know the full story
and, bed-bound and struggling, she couldn't reach
any book that might contain it.

It was like having that broken arm as a child
and a splint that held it up
where she couldn't, therefore,
suck her thumb.

The End of It

Last appointment. The all-clear. The doctor's
painstaking narrative, told to you as if
you'd forgotten the history of your own illness.
Goodbyes. Thanks. Smiles for the nurses
you've seen, on and off, for years now.
On the way out you pause
for a coffee, drink a quiet health
to those in the buzz around you, before it's
out to where smokers huddle, taxis slide to a
stop. Before then you obey the sign:
wash your hands of the place.

Old Marrieds

You crack an egg with more élan:
one quick, deft stroke.
I'm tentative: two, three light taps
then tease apart the
jag-edged halves

but when we kiss
we lean in smooth,
with nothing untoward — who knows
quite how? Just us. But then
our lips are sealed.

Passing Arcadia Close

for my grandson

Outside, it's starless black.
A mile or so away, you're a month old, and I hope,
sleeping, or at least entrancing your tired parents.

To see you, that first time, I'd to take a bus
round the houses, past Arcadia Close,
near the hospitals, gynae- and otherwise.

I recalled the name, from a time before
when I thought I might die before ever having
a grandchild, and could only imagine you, an alien,

beautiful head drifting towards me past the houses,
their windows all respectably curtained. You were amorphous
like a cartoon ghost. Only when I'd held you

did you become substantial to me — though your closed eyes,
your shapely skull, made you even more
like someone who'd arrived from elsewhere, from another planet,
from a long way away, Arcadia, even.

***

Arcadia — we pass it or drift through
before knowing how to recognise the place,
fists curling and uncurling as we try, belatedly,
to grasp anything about it.
                                        I looked up,
from that other bus, years ago, to catch the name,
wondering if fate had played some sort of cruel joke
or if a benevolent God had set it there
to reassure, to lure me on
to the hope that one day I would indeed see you,
your starfish hands pointing everywhere at once.

Oversteps Books Ltd

The Oversteps list includes books by the following poets:

David Grubb, Giles Goodland, Alex Smith, Will Daunt, Patricia Bishop, Christopher Cook, Jan Farquarson, Charles Hadfield, Mandy Pannett, Doris Hulme, James Cole, Helen Kitson, Bill Headdon, Avril Bruton, Marianne Larsen, Anne Lewis-Smith, Mary Maher, Genista Lewes, Miriam Darlington, Anne Born, Glen Phillips, Rebecca Gethin, W H Petty, Melanie Penycate, Andrew Nightingale, Caroline Carver, John Stuart, Rose Cook, Jenny Hope, Hilary Elfick, Anne Stewart, Oz Hardwick, Terry Gifford, Michael Swan, Maggie Butt, Anthony Watts, Joan McGavin, Robert Stein, Graham High, Ross Cogan, Ann Kelley, A C Clarke, Diane Tang, R V Bailey, John Daniel, Alwyn Marriage, Kathleen Kummer, Jean Atkin, Charles Bennett, Elisabeth Rowe, Marie Marshall, Ken Head, Robert Cole, Cora Greenhill, John Torrance, Michael Bayley, Christopher North, Simon Richey, Lynn Roberts, Sue Davies, Mark Totterdell, Michael Thomas, Ann Segrave, Helen Overell, Rose Flint, Denise Bennett, James Turner, Sue Boyle, Jane Spiro, Jennie Osborne, John Daniel, Janet Loverseed, Wendy Klein, Sally Festing, Angela Stoner, Simon Williams, Susan Taylor, Richard Skinner and Fokkina McDonnell.

For details of all these books, information about Oversteps and up-to-date news, please look at our website and blog:

www.overstepsbooks.com
http://overstepsbooks.wordpress.com